Annulment in the Philippines

-

How to end a bad Marriage

Arthur Crandon LL.B. (Hons), M.A.

Annulment in the Philippines

Copyright Arthur Crandon 2024

All rights reserved. No part of this book may be reproduced, stored in a retrieval system, or transmitted in any form or by any means—electronic, mechanical, photocopying, recording, or otherwise—without the prior written permission of the publisher, except for brief quotations in critical reviews or articles.

This is a work of fiction. Names, characters, places, and incidents are either the product of the author's imagination or used fictitiously. Any resemblance to actual persons, living or dead, events, or locales is entirely coincidental.

ISBN: 9798335152594

Cover design by Lance Ceniza

Interior design and formatting by Lynnie Ceniza

Published by Arthur Crandon Publishing

Visit our website: Arthurcrandon.co.uk

DISCLAIMER

The information provided in this book is for general informational purposes only. It does not constitute legal, financial, or professional advice. While every effort has been made to ensure accuracy, the author and publisher assume no responsibility for errors or omissions. Readers should consult with appropriate professionals for specific advice tailored to their individual circumstances.

First Edition: July 2024

Visit Arthurcrandon.co.uk for More Titles

See more books to help you in the Philippines on

www.arthurcrandon.co.uk

CONTENTS

1 What is the difference?   1

2 The Process explained   5

3 Alternatives   11

4 The Future   15

5 History of Annulment   21

BACKGROUND INFORMATION

There are only two countries in the world that do not recognize divorce. The Vatican City, and the Philippines.

What this means in practice, is that failed marriages in the Philippines cannot be dissolved by divorce. There has to be an annulment.

An annulment is a centuries old catholic remedy, whereby, a marriage is not dissolved, it is deemed to have never existed.
It's a complicated process, which can take 2 – 5 years or more, and cost 150,000 php or more, with many court hearings, and fictitious proceedings.

Unless the girl is living abroad (say Hong Kong) she will not be able to do a divorce – she is stuck with trying to get an annulment – most cannot afford the process.

1 WHAT IS THE DIFFERENCE?

In the Philippines, the concepts of annulment and divorce are distinct and governed by different legal frameworks. Here's a detailed explanation of each:

Annulment

Definition: Annulment is a legal procedure that declares a marriage null and void from the beginning. It means that, in the eyes of the law, the marriage never legally existed.

Grounds for Annulment: The grounds for annulment include:

-

Lack of parental consent (if either party was between 18 and 21 years old at the time of marriage)

Psychological incapacity

Fraud

Force, intimidation, or undue influence

Impotence

Sexually transmitted disease

Effects: Once an annulment is granted, it is as if the marriage never happened. This can affect issues like property division and child legitimacy

Divorce

Definition: Divorce is the legal dissolution of a valid marriage. It ends the marriage and allows both parties to remarry.

Current Status in the Philippines: As of now, the Philippines does not generally permit divorce for non-Muslim citizens. The only exception is for Filipino Muslims under the Code of Muslim Personal Laws.

Grounds for Divorce (for Muslims): Grounds include habitual physical violence, abandonment, imprisonment for more than six years, and irreconcilable differences

Effects: Divorce legally ends the marriage, and the court may resolve issues such as child custody, division of assets, and spousal support.

Key Differences

Legal Recognition: Annulment treats the marriage as if it never existed, while divorce ends a legally valid marriage.

Availability: Annulment is available to all citizens under specific grounds, while divorce is only available to Filipino Muslims

Impact on Children and Property: Annulment can complicate issues related to child legitimacy and property division, as the marriage is considered void from the start.

Divorce, on the other hand, allows for a more straightforward resolution of these issues[1]

Understanding these differences is crucial for anyone considering changes in their marital status in the Philippines.

2 THE PROCESS EXPLAINED

The annulment process in the Philippines is a legal procedure that declares a marriage null and void, as if it never existed. Here's a detailed explanation of the steps involved:

Consultation with a Family Lawyer

Initial Meeting: It's crucial to consult with an experienced family lawyer who specializes in annulment cases. They will help you understand the grounds for annulment and guide you through the legal process.

Grounds for Annulment

Psychological Incapacity: One or both parties are unable to fulfill the basic obligations of marriage due to psychological issues.

Fraud: Deception that led to the marriage, such as lying about being pregnant or concealing a drug addiction.

Lack of Parental Consent: If either party was between 18 and 21 years old at the time of marriage without parental consent.

Force, Intimidation, or Undue Influence: If one party was forced or threatened into the marriage.

Impotence: Inability to consummate the marriage.

Sexually Transmitted Disease: If one party had a serious, incurable STD at the time of marriage.

Preparation of the Petition

Document Preparation: Your lawyer will help you prepare the Petition for Annulment, which includes details about your marriage, the specific ground for annulment, and supporting evidence.

Filing the Petition

Court Submission: The petition is filed in the appropriate Regional Trial Court (RTC). The court assigns a docket number and schedules hearings.

Court Proceedings

Hearings: The court conducts several hearings to evaluate the evidence and arguments presented by both parties. This may involve presenting witnesses, experts, and documentary evidence.

Psychological Evaluation: In cases of psychological incapacity, a psychological evaluation may be required.

Decision and Annulment Decree

Court Decision: After the hearings, the court renders a decision based on the evidence and applicable laws. If the annulment is granted, the court issues an Annulment Decree, declaring the marriage null and void. Success is not guaranteed. There is a government lawyer in the court whose job it is to object to the granting of the petition if they can

Registration

Updating Records: The Annulment Decree must be registered with the Local Civil Registrar and the Philippine Statistics Authority (PSA) to update your marital status.

Additional Considerations

Time and Cost: The annulment process can be lengthy and expensive, often taking several months to years to complete.

Emotional Impact: Annulment can be emotionally challenging. It's important to seek support from family, friends, or a counselor during this time.

Each annulment case is unique, and the specific steps and requirements may vary depending on the circumstances. Consulting with a professional legal advisor is essential to navigate the process effectively.

3 ALTERNATIVES

In the Philippines, there are a few alternatives to annulment that can allow a married person to remarry. Here are the main options:

Declaration of Nullity of Marriage

Definition: This legal process declares a marriage void from the beginning (void ab initio). Unlike annulment, which applies to voidable marriages, a declaration of nullity applies to marriages that were never valid.

Grounds: Grounds include bigamous marriages, underage marriages without proper consent, and marriages where one party was psychologically incapacitated at the time of marriage.

Legal Separation

Definition: Legal separation allows spouses to live separately and divide their property but does not dissolve the marriage. Therefore, it does not permit remarriage.

Purpose: It is an option for those who cannot or do not want to pursue annulment but wish to live separate lives.

Recognition of Foreign Divorce

Eligibility: This is applicable if one spouse

is a foreigner and obtains a divorce in their home country. The Filipino spouse can then file for recognition of the foreign divorce in the Philippines.

Process: The Filipino spouse must file a petition in a Philippine court to recognize the foreign divorce decree.

Presumption of Death

Definition: If a spouse has been absent for four consecutive years and is presumed dead, the remaining spouse can file a petition for a declaration of presumptive death.

Effect: Once granted, the remaining spouse is free to remarry. If the presumed dead spouse reappears, the subsequent marriage is automatically terminated.

Important Considerations

Legal Advice: It's crucial to consult with a family lawyer to understand the best option based on individual circumstances.

Documentation: Proper documentation and legal procedures must be followed to ensure the validity of any action taken.

Each of these alternatives has specific legal requirements and implications. Consulting with a legal professional can provide personalized guidance and help navigate the complexities of Philippine family law.

# 4 THE FUTURE

The future of annulment and divorce in the Philippines is a topic of ongoing debate and potential legislative change. Here are some possible scenarios:

Introduction of Divorce Legislation

Current Status: The Philippines is one of the few countries without a divorce law for non-Muslim citizens.

Potential Changes: There have been several attempts to introduce divorce legislation. If passed, this would allow couples to legally dissolve their marriages, similar to other countries.

Grounds for Divorce: Proposed grounds for divorce include irreconcilable differences, domestic abuse, and separation for a specified period.

Expansion of Annulment Grounds

Current Grounds: Annulment is currently based on specific grounds such as psychological incapacity, fraud, and lack of parental consent.

Potential Changes: Future legislation could expand the grounds for annulment to make it more accessible. This might include broader definitions of psychological incapacity or additional grounds like chronic substance abuse.

Simplification of Legal Procedures

Current Process: The annulment process is often lengthy and expensive, involving multiple court hearings and extensive documentation.

Potential Changes: Simplifying the legal procedures for annulment and divorce could make these processes more efficient and less burdensome. This might include streamlined court procedures or alternative dispute resolution mechanisms.

Recognition of Foreign Divorces

Current Status: Currently, only divorces obtained by Filipino citizens married to foreigners are recognized.

Potential Changes: Future legislation might allow for broader recognition of foreign divorces, making it easier for Filipinos who have divorced abroad to remarry in the Philippines

Enhanced Support Services

Current Support: Limited support services are available for individuals undergoing annulment or legal separation.

Potential Changes: Future scenarios could include enhanced support services such as counseling, legal aid, and financial assistance for those affected by marital dissolution.

Cultural and Social Shifts

Current Attitudes: Cultural and religious beliefs strongly influence attitudes towards marriage and divorce in the Philippines.

Potential Changes: As societal attitudes evolve, there may be greater acceptance of divorce and annulment, leading to increased legislative support for these options.

Conclusion

The future of annulment and divorce in the Philippines will likely involve a combination of legislative changes, procedural reforms, and shifts in cultural attitudes. These changes aim to provide more accessible and fair options for individuals seeking to dissolve their marriages.

5 A HISTORY OF ANNULMENT

Annulment is a legal procedure that declares a marriage null and void, as if it never existed. The concept of annulment has evolved over centuries and varies across different cultures and legal systems.

Here's a detailed history of annulment worldwide:

Ancient and medieval times

Early civilizations: in ancient civilizations, marriage was often seen as a contract, and annulments were rare. Marriages could be dissolved for reasons such as infertility or failure to produce heirs.

Christianity's influence: with the advent of christianity, marriage began to be viewed as a sacred and indissoluble union. The catholic church played a significant role in shaping the concept of annulment. Early church councils established grounds for annulment, such as consanguinity (being closely related) and coercion.

Middle ages

Canon law: during the middle ages, the catholic church developed a detailed system of canon law governing marriage and annulment. Grounds for annulment included lack of consent, impotence, and pre-existing marriage.

Notable cases: one of the most famous annulment cases was that of king henry viii of England, who sought an annulment from Catherine of Aragon. When the pope refused, henry broke away from the catholic church and established the church of England.

Modern era

Catholic church: the catholic church continues to have a formal annulment process, which involves a tribunal that examines the validity of the marriage. Grounds for annulment included, fraud and lack of consent.

Protestant reformation: the protestant reformation led to different views on marriage and annulment. Many protestant denominations do not have a formal annulment process and instead allow for divorce.

Secular legal systems

Civil annulments: in secular legal systems, annulments are granted based on specific legal grounds, such as bigamy, underage marriage, and fraud. Unlike divorce, annulment is retroactive, meaning the marriage is considered invalid from the start.

Global variations: different countries have varying laws regarding annulment. For example, in the United States, annulment laws vary by state, while in the Philippines, annulment is the primary means of dissolving a marriage due to the lack of a divorce law for non-muslims.

Recent developments

- **Pope Francis' reforms**: in 2015, pope Francis introduced reforms to streamline the catholic annulment process, making it quicker and less costly. These reforms aimed to make annulment more accessible to Catholics worldwide.

- **Legal and social changes**: as societal attitudes towards marriage and divorce evolve, there have been calls for more accessible and fair annulment processes. Some countries are considering or have implemented reforms to simplify the annulment process.

Conclusion

The history of annulment reflects the

evolving views on marriage, influenced by religious, cultural, and legal factors. While the concept of annulment has ancient roots, modern legal systems continue to adapt to changing societal norms and values.

Visit Arthurcrandon.co.uk for More Titles

ABOUT THE AUTHOR

Arthur Crandon is a retired lawyer and a prolific writer. Hi is British and grew up in a rural community in Somerset. He has lived in England, Wales, Hong Kong and the Philippines and now spends most of his time in the Philippines with his Visayan wife and their son.

He loves to hear from anyone who has anything to do with the Philippines – you can email him anytime on:

ac@arthurcrandon.co.uk

www.ingramcontent.com/pod-product-compliance
Lightning Source LLC
Chambersburg PA
CBHW072049230526
45479CB00009B/334